All rights reserved, no part of this publication
may be either reproduced or transmitted
by any means whatsoever without the
prior permission of the publisher.
Text and images © Charlotte Moore

GINGER FYRE PRESS
Gingerfyrepress.com
Typesetting © Ginger Fyre Press March 2021
Ginger Fyre Press is an imprint of Veneficia Publications

The Life of a Honeybee

Written and Illustrated by Charlotte Moore

This book belongs to ...

....

Hello, my name is Heather. Come and join me on a journey through my life . . .

One warm, sunny day, and in a hive, high up in a hollow tree, the Queen Bee, mother of all bees laid her eggs.

Each egg was as tiny as a grain of rice.

HONEYBEE FACTS

There is only one Queen Bee that lives in the hive. Her job is to lay the eggs. The Queen Bee will be 2cm in length, and unlike most bees, which only live up to 6 weeks during the summer, the Queen Bee can live up to 5 years.

During the winter months, the Queen Bee does not lay any eggs, and the worker bees that are born in the autumn will live until the following spring.

A few days later, the Queen Bee's eggs began to hatch. The little bee who hatched first was amazed at all the sights around her.

Then the little bee was given her very own name, Heather the Honeybee. Heather was curious and couldn't wait to explore her home. But Heather was far too little and needed to be looked after by the worker bees called Brood nurses.

HONEYBEE FACTS

Bees known as Brood nurses help to look after the baby bees, called larvae, in the Nursery made of honeycomb cells.

The new larvae need to be fed constantly to help with their quick growth and development. If there are new Queen Bees, queen larvae will float on a sea of sugary bee gland, known as royal jelly. The future worker bees however will eat a beebread which is a mix of fermented pollen and honey.

Before long, Heather had grown strong enough and no longer needed to be looked after by the Brood nurses. She could now start the work that every other bee does in the hive.

The first job for being a worker bee is a Cleaner. So, Heather was taken to the cells of the hive where she saw other bees cleaning, sweeping, and washing away all the unwanted bits and pieces.

HONEYBEE FACTS

For the first 2 days of a bee's life, they will have the job of being a Cleaner, which involves cleaning cells, including the one from which they hatched, and they help make sure that the hive stays fresh as well as removing any bees that have died.

They will also make sure that all of the waste that the Queen Bee creates is disposed of.

3 days passed and it was now time for Heather to move onto her next job, which was to be a Brood nurse.

She was told that she will have the job of looking after the new baby bees and making sure that the oldest and youngest baby bees were fed and cleaned. Heather loved this job and smiled as she cared for the babies.

HONEYBEE FACTS

When a bee is 3 days old, they will be given the job of being a Brood nurse, for 3 – 11 days, feeding the oldest and youngest larvae.

All the new larvae will be given a special royal jelly, which is a milky secretion which is 67% water, 12.5% proteins, 11% sugar, 6% fatty acids, and 3.5% amino acids.

This is not given to the new developing Queen Bees, and in order for bees to become Queen Bees, the future queens will only be fed pollen and honey.

Heather had such a lovely time looking after the baby bees, but before she knew it, she was 11 days old. She had reached the end of her time of looking after the bees that she had grown very fond of.

So, she moved onto the next job, where she would learn how to make beeswax and build the honeycomb, using the new nectar that had been brought in by the Harvester bees.

She even used some special nectar, to help close-up where a new egg had been laid.

HONEYBEE FACTS

Once a bee has reached the end of being a Brood nurse, they will then learn how to make beeswax and build comb, both for the cells for new eggs and for the cells to store honey, which is what bees eat.

Bee's wax is a sugary liquid that oozes through the bee's small pores on their abdomens. The worker bees will then chew the wax until it becomes soft. The workers will then use their wings to fan the wax dry and hard to add to the construction of the honeycomb. Bees will keep this job until they are 17 days old.

Heather enjoyed creating the honeycomb and wax, but as many more days went by, she was older and stronger, and she could now become a Guard bee, Guarding the hive.

This then allowed her to see the world just outside as well as protecting her home.

So, before beginning her new job, Heather was told about all the enemies to the hive and that her job was to fight off incoming threats to the hive like Hornets.

HONEYBEE FACTS

After 17 days, bees will be given the job of being a Guard bee.

This job is to help protect the hive from any possible threats and enemies. Bees will fly a certain distance until they know that it is safe to stop chasing their enemy before they return to the hive.

Before Heather knew it, she was old enough to leave the nest and she was given a more important job. She was to be a Scout bee.

Heather was told before she left the hive, to remember what she passes, so later she will be able to return home.

Heather was even told about all the dangers to a Honeybee too. Outside, the safety of the hive there are bigger animals like birds that are not friendly to bees, trying to eat them all up!

HONEYBEE FACTS

When a bee is 22 days old, it will be strong enough and big enough to leave the hive as a Scout bee. A Scout bee has the job of finding new flowers, especially if there is now a new colony of bees that have moved on from the old hive. When a Scout bee has found new flowers, and for them to collect nectar as well as food, the Scout bee will return to the hive and perform a dance called a Waggle dance.

A Waggle dance is a bee's way of talking to other bees and as well as using the Waggle dance, the Scout bee uses the sun's position as a guide.

Soon it was time for Heather to be given the most important job of them all – collecting nectar and pollen from the flowers.

As Heather arrived at a colourful meadow, full of beautiful flowers, with the other Harvester bees, Heather could not wait to start collecting the nectar.

As Heather flew closer to a nearby flower, the little bee giggled as a petal tickled her face. This was how the flower welcomed Heather, as it opened its petals. Using her long tube – like tongue, she sipped up the sweet runny liquid called nectar.

HONEYBEE FACTS

The final job of being a worker bee is the most important job of all – a Harvester bee.

After receiving the Waggle dance directions from the Scouts, the Harvester bees will then fly off to harvest the newly found food supplies.

Harvester bees will be responsible for sipping up the nectar to take back to the hive, which will then be turned into honey.

"Mmm, this is delicious." Heather said, just as another Harvester bee passed by.

"Don't take too much Heather. We may be the biggest out of all of the worker bees now, but there is a limit to how much we can sip." The Harvester bee said as Heather then flew on to another flower.

Heather knew that the bee was right, but it was so tasty.

HONEYBEE FACTS

Other than their long tube – like tongues, to help sip up the nectar, bees have two stomachs – one to store the nectar and one to store their food.

As Heather continued to fly from flower to flower, she even met an insect that was not a bee at all. This insect, and its colourful wings was called a butterfly.

"You're so beautiful, just like a flower." Heather said with a smile. Then after the butterfly thanked her, Heather and the butterfly quickly became friends.

HONEYBEE FACTS

Bees are the largest pollen and nectar collectors, but there are also other insects such as butterflies which also collect nectar.

Bees and butterflies are often found in the same meadow and are friendly to one another.

As soon as Heather had finished gathering all the nectar, and all that she could carry, she said goodbye to the butterfly and headed back to the hive, after a hard day's work.

"Mmm, nectar is delicious. I can't wait to do this again tomorrow, and to see my butterfly friend." Heather said with a smile.

HONEYBEE FACTS

In one single journey to and from the hive, a bee will visit between 50 and 100 flowers and will come back to the hive, carrying more than half her weight in pollen. The leftover pollen, which is brought back to the hive, is taken from the bee's body by babysitter bees that mix it with the honey, to feed the baby bees.

Every time a bee collects nectar, and flies to flower to flower, small grains of dust called pollen, stick to the bee's little furry body. Then it comes off to create new flowers and the food we eat.

Back inside the hive, Heather and the Harvester bees return and pass their nectar to the other Brood nurses. This will then over time, turn into liquid gold honey, for the bees to eat.

The Brood nurses even allowed Heather to visit her favourite place in the hive, the Nursery. This was because she had pollen grains still stuck to her furry body.

What a lovely day it had been for Heather, and she couldn't wait to continue collecting the pollen and helping to feed the baby bees for the rest of her little life.

HONEYBEE FACTS

Due to being the final stage that a worker bee will have, a bee will keep their job as a Harvester which is from 22 days up until they die. This is the life cycle of a worker bee as well as growing from a larva to a pupa and then into a full-grown adult.

The End

www.ingramcontent.com/pod-product-compliance
Lightning Source LLC
Chambersburg PA
CBHW041820080526

44588CB00004B/65